Telling It All: Trauma And the Unspeakable Truths

Jenna Casey

BookLeaf
Publishing

India | USA | UK

Telling It All: Trauma And the Unspeakable
Truths © 2024 Jenna Casey

Presentation by *BookLeaf Publishing*

Web: www.bookleafpub.com

E-mail: info@bookleafpub.com

ISBN: 9789360942830

First edition 2024

Slapskickspuncheswhips

Slaps kicks punches whips
Bruises to hide, scars explained
Laugh to hide the pain
Wondering out loud some days
Will life always be this way?

Uncomfortable Skin

Uncomfortable
Shame in my own skin
Memories I hide
Overexposed body…
Mutilate…no value

Inappropriate

Witnessing adults
In adult activities
Confusion, regret
The inappropriate deed
Pretending I didn't see

Old Wounds

Teenage pregnancy
The first tale of temptation
Now ending in tears
The choice of termination
Stirrups left holding my pain

Untitled Assault

5

Nonconsensual
I had a right to say no
The violation
The crime was taking my voice
The choice to forgive myself

Blue (Intimate Partner Violence)

B- Blows to my head and now I'm bruised

L- Love shouldn't hurt

U- Unlikely to tell a soul of these tales

E- Equally feeling love and hate for you leaves me confused

Broken (Infertility, Pregnancy Loss)

B - Babies r everywhere

R- Releasing guilt, shame, despair

O- Only God knows the time and place

K- Keeping faith but frustrated

E- Enduring constant reminders of something so commonplace of which I am unable to escape

N- A dream deferred, neverending heartache

Reclaiming the Body

Reclaiming the Body is about increasing body awareness and feelings toward the body that are often impacted by trauma, releasing stored memories, and fostering compassion to the body and self.

Mindful Release

I place it over my heart
I breathe in new air
Breathe out toxic energy
Master of body and thoughts

Quote

"I am more than what has happened to my body"

The Empty Seat

An absent parent
Haunts me from an empty seat
A dark legacy
Anger, Self-doubt, and Mistrust
Leaving me more than you gave

Improper Care

I needed you when you left me home alone.
I needed you when you sent me to school
disheveled and dirty.
I needed you when taking care of my siblings
was too much for my juvenile mind to
comprehend.
I needed you to take care of me.
I needed you to provide for me.
I needed you to tell me I'm worthy of love.
I needed you to tell me its not my fault you did
not provide me enough.

Dad's Weekend

On Dad's weekend everything goes my way.
But it doesn't matter.
My world has been shattered.
I lost my sense of trust.
My parents' divorced and I lost my center.
Picking sides in a futile battle.
There is no winner.
On Dad's weekend.

Grief and loss

Reminders of you everywhere.
Pain never-ending.
Heartache that won't subside.
Gaping hole in my heart.
I miss you.

PTSD

P- Preparing
T- Terrified
S- Scars and All
D- Determined

Divorce

D- Death
I- Independence
V- Vulnerability
O-Opposition
R-Recovery
C- Creating A New Future
E- Energy Release

Reclaiming the Mind

Reclaiming the mind is about relieving responsibility for trauma we have encountered, reintroducing feelings of trust, and instilling hope for the future.

Mindful Release

Breathing in and out
Imagine a healing light
I can feel the glow
Cold pebbles beneath my toes
Loving kind thoughts follow me

Quote

"I deserve peace of mind and happiness"

Types of Trauma

Trauma discussed in this work include:

Reclaiming the Body collection:
Childhood physical Abuse
Inappropriate touch and Other inappropriate childhood activities
Teen Abortion
Assault
Partner violence
Infertility and pregnancy loss

Reclaiming the Mind Collection
Childhood Abandonment
Childhood Neglect
Childhood divorce
Divorce
Grief/loss
PTSD

Resources

Crisis and Trauma Resource Institute

The National Child Traumatic Stress Network

9 789360 942830